GROGAN'S

100 Best Cartoons

DOUBLE
STOREY
a juta company

ACKNOWLEDGEMENTS

With thanks to the Cape Times and Sunday Independent,
where these cartoons first appeared

First published 2003 by Double Storey Books,
a Juta company, Mercury Crescent, Wetton, Cape Town

© 2003 Tony Grogan

ISBN 1-919930-01-9

Page layout by Claudine Willatt-Bate
Cover design by Abdul Amien
Printing and binding by ABC Press, Epping, Cape Town

FOREWORD

Cartooning, I imagine, is similar to lyric writing, in that it is essentially the art of the idea. And like lyric writing, it is a process of elimination, removing all that is unnecessary in order to reveal the essence of the subject in a surprising way. A cartoonist, unlike an artist, does not have the luxury of drawing that which he sees before him, but is faced with a blank sheet of paper and the need for a brilliant idea. An insight as opposed to a point of view.

It is not just enough to describe a funny situation in order to create a joke. A joke needs a set-up – familiar points of reference and a payoff that surprises and reveals a truth which seems obvious only after it has been revealed.

Cartoons are strange in the way that lyrics are strange. Cartoons use devices like exaggeration and distortion in the way that lyrics use rhyme and meter. It is this unnaturalness, this strangeness that allows the humorist to say or draw things that might be embarrassing if presented in a normal fashion. As Saul Steinberg says, humour is a device to clothe reality so that it will be 'forgiven'.

I have always thought of Tony as brilliant and am filled with admiration when I consider the intimidating challenge of his art. It is one thing to write a popular song now and again, but to produce on a daily basis the quality of work that Tony has done for the past twenty years is astounding, and this volume is proof of that. Through the art of this strange form he has surprised us, amused us, provided us with insight and revealed that which we may have been aware of but couldn't see.

David Kramer

1974   "Just stand up every now and then and shout 'Vrystaat', and they'll never know we're from the British Embassy."

The British Lions rugby team, ignoring a ban on sporting links with South Africa, toured the country to the displeasure of Prime Minister Harold Wilson, who ordered diplomatic staff in South Africa not to attend any matches. This was my first cartoon for the *Cape Times*.

1975   Prime Minister John Vorster's futile attempts to hold back the course of history.

2

1976   The reforms of apartheid made by Vorster's government were painfully slow and hesitant.

1977   Showing typical bravado, the Nationalist government announced that its course was fixed, determined and certain.

11 November 1977   "Ja, you haf' strong aggressive tendencies, an inclination to impulsiveness, a deep-seated sense of insecurity und zis bump tells me … ja, zis bump tells me you have recently bumped your own head against a vall."

Minister of Justice Jimmy Kruger was widely condemned for his callous response to the death of Steve Biko, after saying that it left him cold and that Biko had hit his head against a wall in frustration at being arrested.

1978

"Another cup of tea, sir?"

Minister Connie Mulder tried to make light of the Information Scandal by describing it as a storm in a teacup.

30 January 1979   At a time when love across the colour line was unlawful, a concerned reader drew my attention to a disturbing development in the cartoon strip *Dr Kildare* when the white doctor fell in love with a beautiful Indian colleague.

8 May 1979   Prime Minister P.W. Botha's tentative reforms aroused the consternation of arch-conservative Andries Treurnicht.

1979   Even within the Nationalist government there were varying opinions on the pace of change.

Once upon a time there was a beautiful verkrampte princess who went to bed with a handsome prince, but when she awoke she discovered that the fair young prince had turned into a Prog.

1979   Tensions mounted between P.W. Botha and Andries Treurnicht as the Prime Minister continued to tout reform.

12 March 1980

When political unrest broke out in many townships, the government put the blame on malcontents and provocateurs instead of on its own policies.

1981   As unrest spread throughout the country, it was suggested that white schoolboys be encouraged to join the police reserve.

18 March 1983   One of the worst sins in apartheid South Africa was conscientious refusal to serve in the Defence Force.

1983

To persuade the white electorate to approve a new constitution that would extend limited rights to coloureds and Indians, the Nationalist government embarked on a massive media campaign.

1983   Dr Andries Treurnicht ("Dr No") was not impressed by the proposed new constitution.

NATURE NOTEBOOK

THE CRESTED DRAADSITTER (Inanus copoutus)

A COMMON RESIDENT SPECIES INHABITING HIGH-LYING AS WELL AS LOW-LYING AREAS FROM THE CAPE TO THE LIMPOPO. A SLUGGISH BIRD WITH GLASSY EYES, IT IS A PER- -ENNIAL HIBERNATOR THAT PERCHES IN ROWS ON LOFTY FENCES, SELDOM ALIGHTING OR FLYING OFF IN ANY DIRECTION. ORNITHOLOGISTS ARE UNCERTAIN WHETHER THE CRESTED DRAADSITTER CAN FLY AT ALL. SO IS THE CRESTED DRAAD- SITTER. IT HAS A VERY CHARACTERISTIC SONG -- A MONOTONOUS PIPING WARBLE RE- -PEATED AT LONG INTERVALS -- 'EK-WIL-NIE, EK-KANNIE' OR OCCASIONALLY 'EK-KANNIE-CARE-LESS'.

GROGAN '83

1983   Most whites were either uncertain about the prospects of reform or indifferent to them.

4 March 1982

The siting of South Africa's first nuclear power station near Cape Town
evoked huge protest despite the promise of cheap electricity.

1985

Hailed in advance as a Rubicon speech, P.W. Botha's tirade ended as a disaster:
overseas banks withdrew their credit and the rand sank in value.

24 May 1985

"Just as I thought! You appear to be suffering from a credibility gap."

After various denials about South African military adventures in foreign territory, many
became sceptical about the utterances of Defence Minister Magnus Malan.

19

28 July 1985

An earthquake in the north of the country prompted this parallel with the voteless black masses flexing their muscles at a time of massive civil unrest.

19 June 1986

"Take him away! He's made a picture of the security forces in action."

Under the state of emergency imposed in the mid-1980s,
photographing the security forces in action was forbidden.

9 April 1987   Government-supporting newspapers were congratulated for reproducing "His Master's Voice" on the crisis of the day.

The government's propaganda campaign to "win the hearts and minds of the people" proved fruitless.

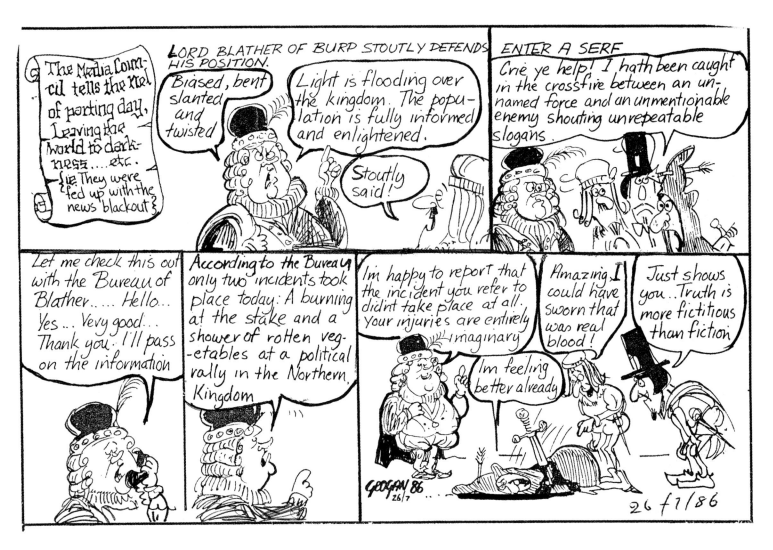

26 July 1986

The government relied on the Bureau of Information to disseminate its benign version
of what was happening in the townships during the state of emergency.

7 May 1986

The actions of the security forces against children in the townships helped drive many residents into the arms of the ANC.

23 January 1987   The Rev. Allan Hendrickse, the first coloured Minister in the Botha government, mistakenly thought his new status would permit him to swim at a whites-only beach – but he was called to heel.

19 August 1988

"Do you *ous* play rugby?"

As the sports boycott of South Africa began to hurt, the President of the South African
Rugby Union travelled the world looking for teams willing to play against the Springboks.

15 June 1991

"So what was it for, Dad?"

9 November 1990

After its unbanning, the ANC was forced by the realities of South Africa
to reconsider some of its long-held policies and dogmas.

8 October 1992   "Look, Mangosuthu, we agree on most things but do we have to take our cultural weeapons to bed with us?"

The insistence of Inkatha that its members be allowed to carry "cultural" weapons was seen by other parties, even its allies like the National Party, as a provocation to violence.

3 September 1992   "How do you say 'a federal system with proportional representation' in Zulu, Van der Merwe?"
The National Party started to look for support from different constituencies.

5 March 1992

It was no longer acceptable to be racist. Even the Conservative Party
tried to distance itself from the racist remarks of the AWB.

8 February 1994

Both F.W. de Klerk and Nelson Mandela claimed responsibility
for having rid South Africa of the far right threat.

3 April 1994

"It's a joy!"

The head of the Independent Electoral Commission, Judge Kriegler, declared
South Africa's first democratic elections substantially fair and free.

6 October 1994

"Give me your huddled millions."

Nelson Mandela undertook a number of visits to the United States to raise
money for programmes to alleviate South Africa's social problems.

14 May 1996

The withdrawal of the National Party under F.W. de Klerk from the Government of National Unity left the ANC with the responsibility of dealing with the country's myriad problems.

1993

"I asked him how to send a registered parcel by priority mail and he said 'Molo'."

After apartheid was scrapped, white civil servants were encouraged to learn a black language.

7 March 1993   "One thing Frikkie can't stand about the Group Areas Act going is having to keep up with the Dlaminis."

8 November 1990

Deprivation caused by apartheid was often cited as a reason for committing crime.

18 May 1994

"As I was saying, affirmative action must not mean that people are moved into jobs beyond their level of competence, like our former chairman, who doesn't seem to have a clue how to pour a cup of tea."

Affirmative action saw many whites, particularly men, finding it difficult to gain employment.

5 May 1995   "Ardent environmentalists, the two of them ... ever since they noticed their beer was clouding up with ore dust."

Despite protests from the environmental lobby, a steel mill was established on the edge of the Langebaan Lagoon.

7 July 1998

"The wife gave me a stark choice: 'Take me,' she said, 'or sport on TV.'"
After the lean years of isolation there was no end to the choice of sport to watch on TV.

10 October 1996

"I ask him what medical aid he belongs to and all I get is a gurgle."

There were shocking stories of private hospitals refusing to admit patients
in extremis unless they could prove their ability to pay.

28 July 1998

"Bertie didn't take any notice of Zuma's health warning on the bottle."

Smokers irked by the Health Minister's obsession with anti-smoking
legislation wondered why she didn't show the same concern with alcohol.

11 March 1999   Minister Jay Naidoo undertook a safari throughout the length of Africa to sell the services of Telkom.

20 November 1998

"At least we've got nice helicopters."

There was widespread protest against the government's plans to spend millions
on purchasing arms when there were far more pressing needs at home.

30 July 1998

While former Nationalist Ministers like Adriaan Vlok accepted responsibility before the TRC for human rights abuses, P.W. Botha remained defiant and unrepentant.

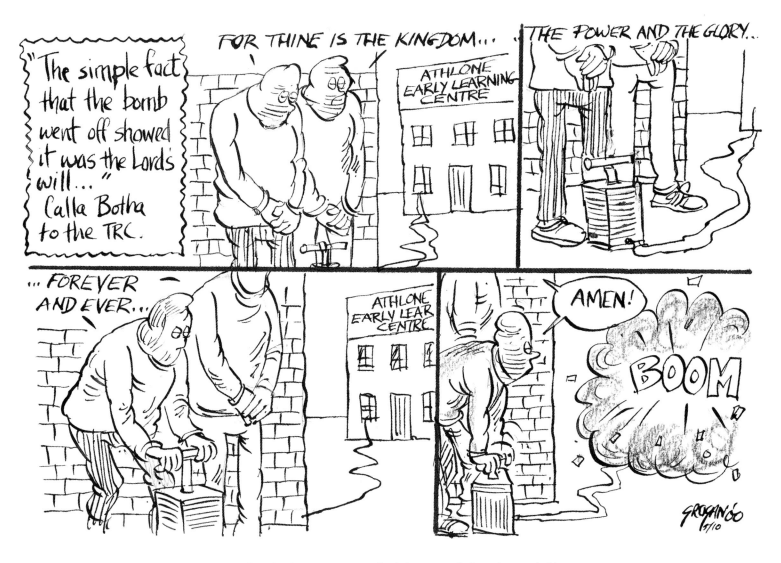

5 October 2000

The ways of the Lord are mysterious indeed if we are to believe the apartheid agent
Calla Botha, who in evidence to the TRC said it was His will that had caused the bomb
Botha had placed at the Athlone Early Learning Centre to explode.

27 November 1998

F.W. de Klerk refused for the most part to admit he had known about human rights abuses
that had taken place under his government or the former of which he was a Minister.

31 October 1998

"Book launch."

There were widely differing responses to the publication of the TRC report.

28 March 2000   Many families of the victims of human rights abuses felt aggrieved by the outcome of the TRC process.

7 September 1998

"Bad news … The rand has crashed against Coca-Cola."

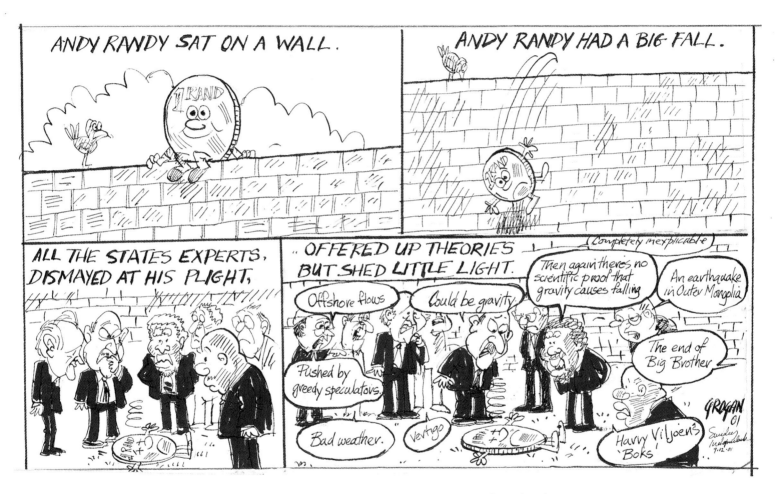

9 December 2001

The decline of the rand against major currencies drew many and varied explanations.

Transylvania Travel Agency

TIPS TO GET ZE MOST OUT OFF YOUR HOLIDAY IN SOUS AFRICA

IF THREATENED BY ZE ROTTVEILER ODER ZE PIT-BULL ON ZE LOOSE, ROLL OVER ON ZE BACK MIT FEET UND HANDS IN ZE AIR TO SHOW ZE PEACEFULNESS UND SUBMISSION. DO NOT LOOK HIM IN ZE EYES BY ANY RESPECTS.

PASOP VIR DIE HOND

VEN PARKIN ZE CAR UND ACCOSTED BY ZE FREELANCE PARKING ATTENDANT, BOW FROM ZE WAISTE DOWN UND COUGH UP ZE HANDSOME TIP OR ELSE HE VILL BE CROSS UND SCRATCH ZE SIDE OF ZE CAR MIT EIN PIECE OFF GLASS.

VEN VALKING IN ZE STREET KEEP ZE EYES DOWNCAST AND ENOUGH MONEY IN ZE POCKETS TO KEEP ZE MUGGERS HAPPY

KEEPING ZE EYES DOWNCAST VILL ALSO HELP TO AVOID STEPPING INTO ZE OPEN MANHOLE VERE DE COVERS HAF BEEN REMOVED FOR SELLING OF ZE SCRAP METAL

IF ZE MINIBUS TAXI SVERVE IN FRONT OFF YOU ON ZE HIGHWAY CAUSING YOU TO LEAVE ZE ROAD UND CRASH INTO ZE TELEPHONE POLE, DO NOT SVEAR OR VAVE ZE FISTS BUT KEEP ZE HEAD DOWN UND EYES DOWNCAST IN CASE YOU UPSET ZE TAXI DRIVER AND HE OPEN FIRE MIT AK-47

OBEY ZESE SENSIBLE TIPS, SHOW ZE DUE HUMILITY UND POLITENESS TO LOCAL CRIMINALS AND YOU VILL HAF A PEACEFUL UND HAPPY HOLIDAY IN ZIS LUFLY COUNTRY.

Danke schön, Help yourself

GROGAN 00

3 March 1992   The soaring crime rate didn't help the tourist industry. Tourists to South Africa were advised, if accosted by muggers, to keep their heads down and eyes averted lest they antagonise their assailants.

15 February 1999

PAC leader Stanley Magoba offered a drastic solution to the soaring crime rate:
hack off the offending limbs of criminals.

11 May 1999

The ineptitude of the police force did not provide much reassurance
to a public trying to cope with the soaring crime rate.

22 December 1999   *"I still feel evolution has a few steps to go before it accomplishes its masterpiece."*

At this time scientists were reported as claiming that evolution had achieved its masterpiece in man.

2 May 2000

"It's the enigmatic smile that puzzles me."
President Thabo Mbeki's utterances and policies on many issues baffled observers.

Mbeki's views on the causes of AIDS were especially controversial.

The President's committee of experts appointed to investigate the causes of AIDS could not find agreement in its report.

12 October 2000

While the President and his Health Minister debated the causes of AIDS,
the toll of people dying from the epidemic continued to rise.

Tannie Evita Bezuidenhout's anti-AIDS campaign was a little too explicit for the SABC.

6 September 2002

The eccentric views of the President and his Health Minister continued to baffle.

18 March 2001

While billions of rands were allotted to arms purchases, the budget
for dealing with AIDS seemed puny in comparison.

10 January 2003   Health Minister Manto Tshabalala-Msimang's remarks on AIDS were frequently bizarre and embarrassing.

27 February 2002

"Meet our new chairman. The ideal choice — very similar to the President's medical adviser, with the added advantage that he's lame."

The departure of Gavin Woods from the chairmanship of the parliamentary committee investigating the government's conduct in the arms deal was widely regretted.

3 October 1999   The Transport Minister's campaign to improve driving on the roads encountered appalling ignorance.

7 February 2000

Justice Minister Penuell Maduna's remarks on rape seemed peculiarly maladroit.

19 July 2001   The government acted forcefully against squatters who occupied land round the cities on which to build homes.

THE AFRICAN JELLYFISH (SADC)

AN INVERTEBRATE WHICH SPINELESSLY FAILS TO STAND UP TO TYRANTS LIKE ROBERT MUGABE.

WOBBLES AT THE FIRST TEST OF ITS PRINCIPLES

SWALLOWS MUGABE'S ARGUMENTS ABOUT SANCTIONS AND LAND-GRABBING HOOK, LINE AND **SINKER**.

VERY SHORT-SIGHTED... CAN'T SEE FURTHER INTO THE FUTURE THAN THE END OF **ITS** NOSE.

16 February 2001   The response of the Southern African Development Community to President Robert Mugabe's increasingly brutal regime seemed timid and short-sighted.

17 June 2002

African heads of state took umbrage at the European Parliament's
stance against President Mugabe of Zimbabwe.

There was even criticism of the media's reporting on Zimbabwe.

13 December 2001   Mugabe's attacks on his political opponents took place against a background of economic crisis.

15 March 2002 While most observers declared the Zimbabwean elections of 2002 neither free nor fair, some African observers, including members of a South African delegation, gave qualified assent.

19 March 2002

"Oh well, I guess boys will be boys."

26 January 2000

"Hello, Alec Erwin? Tell the Greeks we'll compromise. We won't make ouzo so long
as they don't make mampoer, witblits or skokiaan."

The European Community demanded from the Department of Trade and Industry that if South African products
were to be allowed onto the European market, they could no longer carry generic names like sherry and ouzo.

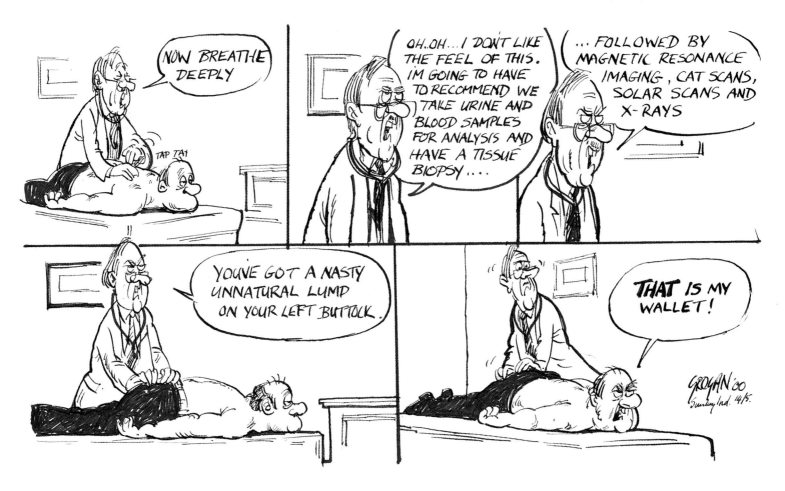

14 May 2000   The costs of medical services for the person in the street continued to rise.

30 October 2001 — In a surprising move, the leader of the New National Party, 'Kortbroek' van Schalkwyk, decided to go for broke and join his party's fortunes in an alliance with the ANC.

2 November 2001   The new alliances must have made former National Party Prime Ministers turn in their graves.

MR PIOUS MHLANGA, LEADER OF THE SOUTH AFRICAN MORAL AND ETHICAL RENEWAL PARTY (SAMERP), WHICH DID NOT DO WELL IN THE 1999 ELECTIONS EXPRESSES HIS OPINION ON THE HARKSEN REVELATIONS:

LOOK AT THIS, HARKSEN SAYS HE GAVE HUGE SUMS OF MONEY TO MORKEL AND MARKOWITZ TOWARDS DA FUNDS

AND THERE'S TALK OF THE ANC RECEIVING FUNDING FROM THAT MAFIA CROOK PALAZZOLO AND TWO INTERNATIONAL PARIAHS, GADDAFI AND SUHARTO.

I AM SHOCKED, ANGRY, ANNOYED, FURIOUS AND BITTERLY DISAPPOINTED!!

WHY DIDN'T WE THINK OF ASKING THEM?

28 May 2002

Jurgen Harksen, a German fugitive from justice, kept Cape Town entertained with his revelations to the Desai commission of inquiry into corruption in local politics.

Crossing the floor legislation allowed the NNP to join in alliance
with the ANC. This was done for the noblest of principles.

8 October 2002   Democratic Alliance members in the Western Cape also prepared to cross to the ANC–NNP majority.

'I weep for you,' the Poacher said
'I deeply sympathize'.
With sobs and tears he sorted out
Those of the largest size,
Holding his pocket handkerchief
Before his streaming eyes.

'O Perlemoen,' the poacher said
'We've made a tidy sum!
Shall we be taking more of you?"
But answer came there none -
And this was scarcely odd, because
They'd plundered every one.

GROGAN '02
With apologies to
Louis Carroll and John Tenniel

6 June 2002   Poaching of perlemoen on the Cape coast threatened the destruction of this resource.

"The lives our distant ancestors led millions of years ago hold a clear lesson for us today: while their footprints on nature were small, ours have become dangerously large" – UN Secretary General Kofi Annan.

"Very nice. Now forget it. Next thing you'll be inventing the motor car and messing up the environment."

"The lone ranger."

22 August 2002

US President George Bush declined to attend the
World Conference on Sustainable Development in Durban.

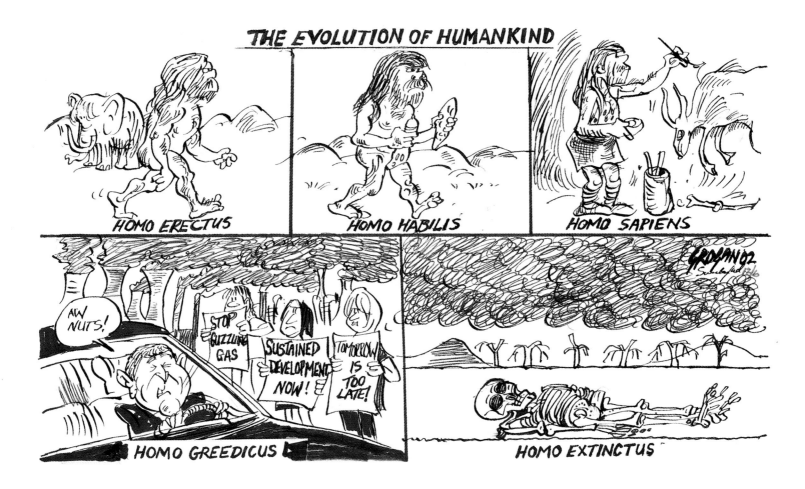

12 June 2002

"The evolution of humankind."

6 September 2002

After all the speeches at the World Conference on Sustainable Development,
one wondered whether much of significance had been accomplished.

28 March 1999

Serbian President Milosevic's defiant response to the West.

9 October 2001

"I don't think that's a Tomahawk you've intercepted. I think it is a bag of maize meal."
The Western Allies dropped food parcels for the Afghan people during the war against the Taliban.

10 April 2002

"Ah'm backin' mah padner Tex Bush in his bid to clean out this li'l ol' world
of all them pesky varmints who's threatening us with terror."

British Prime Minister Tony Blair backed George Bush to the hilt in his "war against terror".

10 July 2002

Many questioned whether the new African Union launched in Durban would be any different from its predecessor, the OAU.

30 October 2002   Deputy Minister Aziz Pahad caused confusion by saying that peer review was not a necessary component of NEPAD (the New Partnership for Africa's Development).

28 July 2002

"Stock response."

The ANC showed a growing tendency to answer criticism
by attaching labels to their critics like Jeremy Cronin.

9 November 2002   The government's softly-softly approach to the Zimbabwe question remained unchanged.

24 October 2002   President Mbeki ordered a new, expensive and (critics said) unnecessary official jet.

19 February 2002

"Spot of labour trouble here. The warders say they're going on strike unless you give them four weeks' leave and a thirteenth cheque."

A commission of inquiry revealed disquieting evidence of warders being paid by prisoners for special favours.

17 July 2002   The Defence portfolio committee reported that many members of the Army were unfit and overweight.

26 November 2002 The Springboks rugby coach, Rudolf Straeuli, came in for flak because of the disastrous performance of his team in an end-of-year tour of France and the UK.